Friends Help Us Over the Potholes On the Road of Life

...and other warm & witty sayings

Words
to
Share

Friends Help Us Over the Potholes On the Road of Life
ISBN 978-0-9828555-1-5

Published by Product Concept Mfg., Inc.
2175 N. Academy Circle #200, Colorado Springs, CO 80909

©2010 Product Concept Mfg., Inc. All rights reserved.

Where quotations do not have a credit, the author is unknown.

Friends
Help Us Over
the Potholes
On the Road
of Life

When the road of life
sends us on detours,
friends show us how
to relax and enjoy
the scenery!

Friends are...
companions in fun,
comfort in sorrow,
defenders in need,
vital to life.

Like branches
of a tree,
we grow in
different directions,
yet our roots
remain as one.
Each of our lives
will always be
a special part
of the other's.

* * * *

If only

I could lift your burden
    and help you up again...

If only

I could part your shadows
    and bring the sunshine in...

If only!

But what I promise you I'll do
    is be here always
        as your friend.

* * * *

A friend is like a mirror,
reflecting back to you the
very best of who you are.

It's Give and Take

Friendship is like a bank account— you can't continue to draw on it without making deposits.

Couldn't Live Without Them!

A friend is a gift
you give yourself.

> - Robert Louis Stevenson

No route is long with
good company.

> - Proverb

Best friend,
my well–spring
in the wilderness!

> - George Eliot

Love is like the
　　wild-rose briar;
Friendship is like
the holly-tree.
The holly is dark
　　when the rose
briar blooms,
But which will bloom
　　　most constantly?

- Emily Brontë

They're the Best

It is better in times of need to have
a friend rather than money.

- Greek proverb

Life has no blessing like a prudent friend.

- Euripides

Your wealth is where your friends are.

- Plautus

The best rule
of friendship
is to keep your

heart

a little softer
than your
head.

People come into your life when you need them.

Some come to offer you guidance toward the next step in your career or for opportunities to develop a skill. Some come when you need a certain kind of encouragement or self-confidence. Still others can offer you spiritual understanding that you need just at that moment in time. Friends come too, to walk the way with you awhile so you can both experience more joy in the journey.

Quality over Quantity

My books and my friends
need only be few...but good.

Many acquaintances will cross your path,
and they may walk with you part of the way...
but those you call your friends
are those who stay
no matter where your road may lead.

Man's best support is a very dear friend.
-Cicero

To Be a Friend

Friendship is equality.
- Pythagoras

There can be no friendship
without confidence,
and no confidence
without integrity.
- Samuel Johnson

Be slow to fall into friendship;
but when thou art in,
continue firm and constant.
- Socrates

Loyalty is what we seek
in friendship.
- Cicero

I can tell who my
  friends are–
they're the ones
   who know my faults
   and are still willing
to be seen with
      me anyway!

Friendship
is what binds
the world
together in peace.

May we all
become friends.

A good friend is like

the sprinkles on ice cream...

the fizz in a cola...

the foam on a latte...

the chocolate on strawberries...

the squiggles on cupcakes...

the whipped cream on brownies...

the frosting on cookies...

... A good friend

is like the big

bright red cherry

on the chocolate

sundae of life!

Hello!

You meet your friend,
your face brightens–
you have struck gold.

- Kassia

Sometimes you know
you've met a lifelong friend
the first time you say Hello.

A friend is, as it were,
a second self.

- Cicero

A friend is one who knows you as you are,
understands where you've been,
accepts who you've become,
and still gently invites you to grow.

What do we live for,
if it is not to make life
less difficult
for each other?

- George Eliot

*   *   *   *

Shared laughter
is the glue
that holds friends
together through
every season
of life.

*   *   *   *

Good Question!

I know you wear
your heart on your sleeve...
but where do you keep your
other body parts?

Do you realize that
STRESSED
spelled backward is
DESSERTS?

Can we make a comeback
if we've never been in the
first place?

Friends are like
two kids on a seesaw...
you go through all the
ups and downs of life,
but everything's OK
because you're together...

*you're
friends.*

Say That Again?

If you can't be kind…
at least be subtle.

If at first you don't succeed…
destroy all evidence that you ever tried.

It goes without saying…
so let it.

He who laughs last…
didn't get the joke.

On the other hand...
is another set of fingers.

He who hesitates...
is probably right.

All is not lost...
but where in the heck is it, anyway?

Two wrongs don't make a right...
but three lefts do.

The happiness of life
is made up of
minute fractions–
the little,
soon-forgotten charities
of a kiss or smile,
a kind look or
heartfelt compliment.

- Samuel Taylor Coleridge

Devoted Friends

I don't mind
"going nowhere"
with you,
as long as we take
an interesting path
to get there.

When you consider how complex we all are as human beings, how needy we are when it comes to what we expect from others or what we hope for from ourselves, it's a wonder that friendship ever really has a chance to find room in our hearts and minds.

Fortunately, our complexity
shapes our need in a way that
causes each one to stand and
stretch and find a hand to
hold and a heart to confide
in. Fortunately, friendship
is almost as necessary
as breathing.

True friendship is a plant
of slow growth and must
undergo and withstand
the shocks of adversity
before it is entitled
to the appellation.

- George Washington

We've been
friends
since we were
just young
sprouts...

And we'll
still be
friends
when we're
older
than dirt!

Three Kinds
of Friends

There are those who make
things happen,
those who watch
things happen,
and those who wonder
what happened.

Longtime Friends

Someday we'll look back
on this and laugh...
Then quickly change
the subject.

Friends are like…
>   tea bags. You don't know
>   how strong they are until
>   they land in hot water.

Friends are like…
>   fudge. Sweet, but nutty, too.

Friends are like…
>   pretzels. Completely twisted
>   at times.

To handle yourself,
use your head.
To handle your friends,
use your heart.

Friends who listen,
help and care
are God's way
of blessing
our lives
with angels.

Handle with Care

Hold a true friend
with both your hands.

- Nigerian Proverb

Go oft to the house
of thy friend,
for weeds choke
the unused path.

- Ralph Waldo Emerson

Unless you bear the
faults of a friend,
you betray your own.

- Publilius Syrus

Let's always keep growing...

but let's never grow apart!

A friend is someone
who understands
your past,
believes in your future,
and accepts you
just the way you are.

Chuckles

My computer crashed,
and now I have no way
of knowing
who my friends are!

If men liked shopping,
they'd call it research.

- Cynthia Nelms

Laughter is like manure
to a farmer-
It doesn't do any good
until you spread it around!

What makes us friends?
It's not a big thing, really...
     more like a gazillion little things!

The best possession
anyone could have
is the heart-to-heart love
of a genuine friend.

Thus nature has
no love for solitude
and always leans,
as it were,
on some support;
and the sweetest
support is found
in the most
intimate friendship.

- Cicero

Friendship is born
at that moment when
one person says to another,
"What! You too?
I thought I was the only one."

- CS Lewis

Friends
are the
sunshine
of life.

- John Hay

With a friend,
it's OK to get the giggles...
share your secrets...
tell your dreams...
because that's what
friendship's all about.

Even if we're
doing nothing at all...

we're doing something
when we're with a friend.

Friends

FRIENDS who knit together
keep each other in the loop…

FRIENDS who quilt together
keep each other in stitches...

FRIENDS who garden together
keep each other blooming…

FRIENDS who walk together
take things in stride.

Grief can take care of itself,
but to get the full value
of a joy you must have
somebody to divide it with.

- Mark Twain

*F*riends help each other
through the big things,
but cherish together
the little things.

You're never alone when you have a friend.

You always know that life cannot take you too far off the course, that unexpected events can't throw you totally, that all your happy news has a place to be shared...yes, when you have a friend, you always have a place to share the best things about you. You're never alone.

Friendship...

You don't have to clean it,
    scrub it, or shine it…
You don't have to reboot it,
    recharge it, or reprogram it…
You don't have to research it,
    document it, or tally it up…

Just enjoy it!

It is one of the
blessings of old friends
that you can afford
to be stupid with them.

- Ralph Waldo Emerson

The fabric of
friendship
is woven in words
and in laughter…
in stories
and in silence…
in good times
and in cherished
memories.

A friend is someone who,
when you're at the end of your rope,
ties a knot so you can hang on.

True friendship
doesn't notice the
passage of time or
the miles that separate
one friend from the
other. For whether two
hours have passed or
two years slipped
away, the
connection remains.

* * * *

Seasons change...
Time goes by...
Friendship remains.

* * * *

The blessing of friendship is in the kindness shared by two hearts that know each other well, hold each other up in prayer, strengthen each other by thoughtful acts of joy, and remind each other of all that is yet to be.

She gives most
who gives with
Joy.

- Mother Teresa

*The most
beautiful moment*
in any friendship is the one
where unspoken glances
tell all that needs to be said,
where a sparkle in the eye
sends the laughter merrily
through every inch of the
spirit and where the right
word, at the absolutely
right time, makes all the
difference.

* * * *

The most wasted day
of all is one without laughter.
- E. E. Cummings

* * * *

Just Because

Because we get the giggles
and laugh until we cry,
And know if someone's hurting,
with just a simple sigh—

Because we get together
and share "remember whens,"
We share the joy of being
the very best of friends!

10 Things Girlfriends Say

10. "Of course it's his fault—
    that goes without saying."

9. "I think some chocolate ice
   cream would solve the problem."

8. "Yes, I believe you know what
   your cat is thinking."

7. "No, you didn't over-react at all.
   He deserved it."

6. "...it's not your body that's a
   problem- they just don't make
   clothes that fit anymore."

5. "Definitely we're ordering dessert."

4. "Of course you should buy those shoes."

3. "Which one? What are you talking about? Buy both!"

2. That's not a wrinkle- it's just a laugh line that shows you have a great sense of humor.

1. Do you need a shoulder to cry on? I'm on my way over right now.

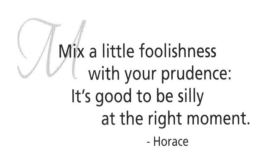

Mix a little foolishness
   with your prudence:
It's good to be silly
   at the right moment.

- Horace

A true friend is the person
who's there for you,
    even though she'd rather
    be someplace else.

Lettuce Always Be Friends!

I can depend on my friends to *turnip*
for me if I'm in a *pickle*...
make *thyme* for me, even when they
have a *bushel* of things to do...
they *squash* my loneliness,
and let me *yammer* on,
even if I don't know *beans*...

Friends give me *peas* of mind,
and I'm *berry* thankful for each one.
As far as I'm concerned,
friends can't be *beet*,
and I'm *plum* happy to have
them in my life
(especially those who laugh
at my *corny* jokes!)

Friendly Advice

"Advice from your friends is like the weather: some of it good, but some of it bad."

I am glad that I paid so little attention to good advice; had I abided by it I might have been saved from some of my most valuable mistakes.

- Edna St. Vincent Millay

He only profits from praise who values criticism.

- Heinrich Heine

Friends are...

the bacon bits in the salad of life...

the cheese in the enchilada of life...

the chocolate chips in the cookie of life!

The smallest
good deed
is better
than
the greatest
intention.

I have no trouble with my enemies.
I can take care of my enemies all right.
But my damn friends...
they're the ones that keep me
walking the floor nights!

- Warren G. Harding

Tsk, Tsk!

"The shortest distance
between two gossips is the
backyard fence."

"I never repeat gossip...
so listen close the first time."

Friends and Family

One loyal friend is worth ten thousand relatives.

- Euripides

"A best friend is the sibling destiny forgot to give you."

"The best kinds of friends are the ones who, over time, seem more like family."

A sympathetic friend can be quite as dear as a brother.

- Homer

Best Friends...

Share the good times
as well as the bad times
with you,

stick around when
everyone else has
walked out on you,

ignore the worst
and bring out the
best in you.

Genuine Friendship

A mere friend will agree
with you, but a real
friend will argue.
- Proverb

"You may be one person
in the world,
but you may be the world
to one person."

A friend is one to whom
one can pour out all
the contents of one's heart,
chaff and grain together,
knowing that the gentlest
of hands will take and sift it,
keeping what is worth keeping,
and, with the breath of kindness,
blow the rest away.

- Proverb

That's Friendship!

Business, you know,
may bring money,
but friendship hardly
ever does.

- Jane Austen

"Love is blind;
friendship closes its eyes."

There is nothing
on this earth more
to be prized than
true friendship.

- Thomas Aquinas

Be slow in choosing friends,
but even slower in changing them.

- Proverb

Friends Are Punny!

A friend who's a baker
has lots of dough.

You'll have a ball
with a friend who bowls.

A friend who gardens
is always down-to-earth.

Life hums right along
when you're with a musician.

Caution!

To keep your friends,
never press SEND
when you're angry.

When angry, count to four;
when very angry, swear.
- Mark Twain

When good cheer
is lacking, our friends
will be packing.

Friends help us cope by...

*L*istening

*S*ympathizing

*S*upporting

*E*mpathizing

Comforting

Encouraging

Inspiring
and gently nudging
us to move forward.

Birds of a Feather

Tell me thy company
and I will tell thee what thou art.

- Cervantes

A man becomes like the
society he loves.

- Proverb

You cannot be friends
upon any other terms
than upon the terms of equality.

- Woodrow Wilson

What draws people
to be friends is that
they see the same truth.

They share it.

One day a traveler came to Socrates and told him he had something to say regarding one of Socrates' dear friends. Before the traveler could begin speaking, however, Socrates asked the man three questions.

"First," Socrates asked, "is the story true?"

"I'm not sure," said the traveler. "Actually, I heard it from someone who heard it from someone else."

"Then," Socrates asked, "is the story kind?"

"No, not really," replied the traveler.

"Finally," Socrates asked, "is it necessary that I hear this story?"

"No, it isn't," the traveler admitted. And the tale stopped there.

In Praise of Friends

The sweetest of all
sounds is praise.

- Xenophon

Appreciation
is a wonderful thing:
it makes what is excellent
in others belong to us as well.

- Voltaire

The brighter your
light shines,
the easier it is
for others to see
what's up ahead.

Friends are those
special people who,
every time you see them,
you just want to run up
and hug them!

Three Reasons Why It's Good to Have Friends

Because it's nice
to be able to call someone...
just because.

Because you need someone
to be there for you when you
want to celebrate...
laugh... or cry.

Because the world needs
fewer strangers in it.

Walking with a friend in the dark
is better than walking alone in the light.

- Helen Keller

A friend is like...

a book you can't
put down because
it's way too interesting...

a day you don't want
to end because you're having
so much fun...

a memory you like
to recall because it
makes you smile...

A friend is like...

a song you listen to
over and over because
you love to sing along...

a TV show you never miss
because you see yourself
reflected in it...

A friend is like...

a dream come true
because you'd never
ever trade a friend
for anything else
in the whole
wide world!

Friendly Words

Friendship requires great communication.

- Francis de Sales

"Stay" is a charming word in a friend's vocabulary.

- Louisa May Alcott

Treat your friends as you do your pictures, and place them in their best light.

- Jennie Jerome Churchill

Some of my friends say
the glass is half empty,
and some of my friends say
the glass is half full.

I say,
"Do you really want to drink that?"

Buddy Bloopers

• Rushing over and giving
  your friend a big hug…
  only to realize it's someone else.

• E-mailing a hush-hush tidbit
  to one friend…and your entire
  address list.

- Starting to introduce your boss to your friend... and forgetting the names of both.

- Serving a steak dinner to your friend...the vegetarian.

- Sharing a funny story with a friend...the same story she told you yesterday.

Good friends create a space
to learn more about you,
to encourage your light to shine,
and help you reach beyond
the places where you're most
comfortable. Good friends know
that there is truly more
to you than meets the eye.
They are there to help you
become visible to yourself.

The world is round
so that friendship
may encircle it.

- Pierre Teilhard de Chardin

Friendship Takes Effort

Wishing to be friends is
quick work, but friendship
is a slow-ripening fruit.

- Aristotle

Friendship is like money,
easier made than kept.

- Samuel Butler

"To have a good friend
is one of the highest
delights of life;
to be a good friend is
one of the noblest
and most difficult
undertakings."

- Anonymous

Not forgiving a friend
is like refusing to apply
the salve that would
heal the wound.
It allows one bad moment
to cancel out years
of happy memories...
it etches a permanent
frown on your face...
and in your heart.

True What They Say

New friends are silver,
but old are gold.

There's no physician
like a true friend.

Who seeks a faultless friend
remains friendless.

A friend in need
is a friend in deed.

One enemy is many,
but a hundred friends too few.

Sudden friendship,
sure repentance.

The company makes the feast.

Four be the things
I am wiser to know:
Idleness, sorrow,
a friend and a foe.

A true friend
is the best possession.

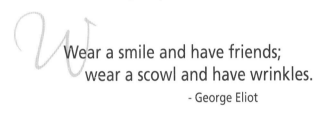

Wear a smile and have friends;
wear a scowl and have wrinkles.

- George Eliot

*Y*ou'll always be my friend-
I've told you *way* too much.

Good friends
are the family
we choose
for ourselves.

Friends with Attitude

"OK, so I'm maladjusted.
But you'll have to admit
I'm a lot of fun."

"Learn from your friends' mistakes,
because you don't have enough time
to make them all yourself."

"Be nice to your friends.
If it weren't for them,
you'd be a total stranger."

"My best friend suffers in silence
louder than anyone I know."

A friend is someone who won't
hesitate to give you a kick in
the pants when you need it...
who won't think twice about
telling you when she thinks
you're making a big mistake...
but who will simply listen
when all you need is a
shoulder to cry on.

A Help in Need

Prosperity makes friends.
Adversity tries them.
- Publilius Syrus

Everyone needs help
from everyone.
- Bertolt Brecht

A friend is never really
known until you call on
her in need.

Even If

A friend
is there for you,
even if you call at
3:00 a.m....

Stands up for you,
even if you've
behaved badly...

Forgives you,
even if you forget to say
"I'm sorry"…

Never says,
"I told you so,"
even if, in fact,
she told you so.

Even where the affections
are not strongly moved by
any superior excellence,
the companions of our
childhood always possess
a certain power over our
minds which hardly any
later friend can obtain.

- Mary Shelley

When things get unraveled,
the threads of friendship
hold us together.

Friends in Deed

Actions, not words,
are the true criterion of the
attachment of friends.
- George Washington

He does good to himself
who does good to his friend.
- Erasmus

My true friends have always
given me that supreme proof of
devotion, a spontaneous aversion
for the man I loved.
- Colette

✳ ✳ ✳ ✳

A friend can see
what's invisible to the eye because
she looks with the heart.

✳ ✳ ✳ ✳

Sometimes I think that friends are like the angels of life who just happen to be human beings. They are the ones who watch over you with a kind of loving and nurturing style that supports the things you do and the hopes and dreams that give meaning to your life. Your angels are always merciful, seeing you with the best possible intentions, holding you in the best possible light.

Friends are angels,
sent to us on the wings
of a blessing.

The glory of friendship
is not the outstretched
hand, nor the kindly
smile, nor the joy of
companionship; it is the
spiritual inspiration that
comes to one when you
discover that someone
else believes in you and
is willing to trust you
with a friendship.

- Ralph Waldo Emerson

There is nothing we like to see so much as the gleam of pleasure in a person's eye when he feels that we have sympathized with him, understood him. At these moments something fine and spiritual passes between two friends. These are the moments worth living.

- Don Marquis

The Friend Inside

Nothing is a greater impediment
to being on good terms with
others than being ill at ease
with yourself.

- Honoré de Balzac

Nobody holds a good opinion
of a man who has a
low opinion of himself.

- Anthony Trollope

Who is no good for herself
is no good for others.

- Proverb

You find yourself refreshed in the presence of cheerful people. Why not make an honest effort to confer that pleasure on others?
Half the battle is gained if you never allow yourself to say anything gloomy.

- Lydia M. Child

How's That Again?

A friend not in need
is a friend indeed.

Do unto others before
they do unto you.

If you can keep your
head while all your friends
are losing theirs,
you are probably clueless.

What Friends Do

Friends are those rare
people who ask how
you are and then wait
to hear the answer.

A true friend helps us
think our best thoughts,
do our noblest deeds,
be our finest selves.

Friends are the ones
who go with you when
the going gets tough.

Isn't it funny how...

...you can spot a friend in a crowd...
before you've even met each other?

...you go shopping together, and she
nabs the perfect outfit for you while
you're still putting your keys in your
purse?

...when you meet with a friend you
haven't seen in 20 years, it feels as if
you're picking up on a conversation
you started yesterday.

...you feel good knowing there's at least one person in the world as crazy as you are?

...you like not having to apologize for getting a case of the sillies from time to time?

...despite all the changes in your lives, despite all the people who have come and gone, your friendship is still going strong?

We are all travellers
in the wilderness of this world,
and the best we can find in our travels
is an honest friend.

- Robert Louis Stevenson

Keep your friends—
they're a whole lot
cheaper than going
to therapy!

Friendship is like that...

The bird, a nest...
the spider, a web...
man, friendship.
- William Blake

Friendship
is a sheltering tree.
- Samuel Taylor Coleridge

Friends are the closest
thing to angels
this side of heaven.

Friends
are for sharing
laughter and sorrows...
joys and complaints...
good times and sad times...
preferably with
plenty
of chocolate!

There is no greater blessing
than a good friend–
except a good friend
who grows to be an
old friend.

Old Friends,
New Friends

Yes'm, old friends is always
best, 'less you can catch a
new one that's fit to make
an old one out of.

- Sarah Orne Jewett

An old friend never can
be found, and nature has
provided that he cannot
easily be lost.

- Samuel Johnson

As in the case of wines
that improve with age, the
oldest friendships ought to
be the most delightful.

- Cicero

True Friends

* * * *

Not everyone you meet becomes a
True Friend, but only a special few.
While you treasure the people who
have come in and out of your life at
various times, True Friends are the
ones who have stayed. They're the
keepers.

You know who they are—
They're the ones who make you
feel valued, important, and unique
(because you are). They're the ones
who make you smile when you meet
them, and it makes your day if, by
chance, you should happen to run
into each other at the coffee shop,
deli, or gym.

When you see their name in your in-box, you click it open, because all the others can wait. When their birthday comes around, you spend hours looking for just the right card, because it has to say just the right thing.

No matter what happens in
life, there's always someone
you can talk to who will listen,
understand, and care.
That's because you have
a True Friend.

*N*ever forget
the days I spent with you.
Continue to be my friend,
as you will always
find me yours.

- Ludwig van Beethoven